ASTRO 2026 SA

MW01478821

.

SAGITTARIUS 2026

INTUITIVE ASTROLOGICAL FORECAST

By Rachel

INTUITIVE ASTROLOGICAL FORECASTS SAGITTARIUS 2026 by RACHEL

2026 : An Unprecedented Celestial Alignment

Gateway to a New Era
An unprecedented cosmic turning point !

Saturn and Neptune merge at the very end of Pisces, a rare event never before experienced in our modern history. This unique conjunction acts as a bridge between the material world and the spiritual world, between the rigor of reality and the infinity of possibilities. Never before have these planets aligned under such an exact configuration, making this period a key moment for both collective and individual evolution.

An Awakening of Ideals and a Profound Restructuring

When Saturn, guardian of time and structures, encounters Neptune, messenger of dreams and transcendence, a deep reorganization of beliefs and values becomes inevitable. This influence urges humanity to review its foundations, to abandon obsolete illusions and to build a future more aligned with principles of wisdom and sustainability.

"Do not dwell in the past, do not dream of the future, concentrate the mind on the present moment." Buddha

Under this exceptional alignment, creativity and spirituality are propelled to unprecedented levels. The artistic, scientific and philosophical realms will be touched by a wave of revolutionary inspiration. Access to new forms of consciousness intensifies, offering the possibility of exploring dimensions until now unsuspected.

A Jupiter–Saturn Trine : The Art of True Balance

Jupiter, the great cosmic amplifier, in perfect harmony with Saturn in Cancer, offers a rare opportunity to reconcile expansion and responsibility. This aspect favors enlightened decision-making, where growth unfolds with wisdom and discernment. It is the time to build ambitious yet realistic projects, to lay down solid foundations for a flourishing future.

"A journey of a thousand miles begins with a single step." Lao Tzu

The Jupiter–Neptune Trine : The Age of Sharing and Benevolence

When Jupiter and Neptune unite under a favorable aspect, humanity is called to rediscover its deeper essence : that of mutual aid and fraternity. This powerful transit inspires us to transcend selfishness and to work for a greater collective good. It is a period when social movements for more justice, equity and solidarity gain in strength and impact.

"You give but little when you give of your possessions. It is when you give of yourself that you truly give." Khalil Gibran

Pluto in Aquarius : An Inevitable Metamorphosis

Pluto, symbol of destruction and rebirth, begins its long journey through Aquarius, initiating a cycle of radical transformation lasting nearly two decades. This transit marks the end of old paradigms and the dawn of an era where technology, collective consciousness and the quest for freedom take on unprecedented momentum. It is an invitation to embrace change without fear, to become the architect of one's own destiny.

"One does not become enlightened by imagining figures of light, but by making the darkness conscious." Carl Jung

The Potentials Offered by this Exceptional Alignment

- **Spiritual Awakening and Access to Higher Consciousness** : A powerful radiance for all signs. A rare opportunity to deepen one's connection with the invisible and to explore new dimensions of being.

- **Accelerated Manifestation of Intentions** : Thanks to the convergence of Neptune and Jupiter, thoughts and emotions aligned with deep aspirations gain amplified power of materialization.

- **Creativity and Innovation** : Fertile ground for scientific discoveries and artistic revolutions, where new forms of expression emerge.

- **Collective Evolution and Redefinition of Values** : A unique chance to build a world based on principles of cooperation, balance and respect for all living beings.

- **Reconnection with Universal Laws** : This astrological passage reminds us that we are co-creators of our reality.

"Do not be satisfied with the stories that have made you who you are. Unfold your own myth." Rumi

2026 is a call to awakening and to action ! It is no longer the time to wait but to embody fully who we are and to dare to create a future worthy of our deepest aspirations.

Major Sagittarius Trends 2026

Expansion of Your Possibilities !

A year of inner growth, structuring decisions and profound relational transformations.

2026 opens before you like a blank book, each page awaiting the imprint of your impulses. A year to believe, to dare, to build with the stars as allies and your inner fire as compass.

A Year of Expansion and Clarification

1. Jupiter at the Helm

Jupiter, your ruling planet, plays a decisive role in widening your perspectives :

- Until June 2, 2026, Jupiter transits Gemini your House VII : partnerships, alliances and commitments (including professional contracts and love relationships) are at the center of your evolution. You attract fruitful collaborations and are called to rethink your relationship with others.

- From June 30, Jupiter enters Leo your House IX : this sector governs higher education, long journeys, spirituality and worldview. It is a powerful call to broaden your horizons, to affirm your truth, to study or to transmit knowledge.

"Success is not the key to happiness. Happiness is the key to success." Albert Schweitzer

Align your heartfelt impulses with your ambitions : it is the right moment to unite passion and vocation.

2. Structure for Endurance

Saturn Gives You Solid Foundations

Saturn, the great teacher, invites you to anchor your projects :

- Until February 14, Saturn is in Pisces — your House IV : it restructures home, roots and intimacy. There may be a move, a family reorganization or a need to redefine what "security" truly means for you.

- From mid-February, Saturn enters Aries your House V : focus turns to creativity, children and love. You are called to give a serious form to your personal expression. Love becomes responsible, and creativity, demanding.

  "Inspiration is a gift. Structure is a choice."

Do not be content to dream : Saturn pushes you to materialize.

3. Uranus, Engine of Change

Uranus transits your House VI (Taurus) until April 25, triggering upheavals in your lifestyle, work environment and even health.

From late April, Uranus enters Gemini your House VII : expect unconventional, surprising yet liberating relationships and partnerships.

"Conscious adaptation is more powerful than instinctive resistance."

Be responsive without freezing. Uranus offers sudden but fertile breakthroughs.

4. Neptune Inspires You

Until January 26, Neptune completes its transit in Pisces House IV : inner life may be unclear but remains fertile. Questions of roots take on a spiritual dimension.

From January 26, Neptune enters Aries your House V : you express your creativity with greater grace, inspiration and idealism. Love may even take on a mystical quality.

"Knowing yourself is the beginning of all wisdom." Aristotle

Let yourself be guided by your inner feelings : your intuition becomes your compass.

5. Pluto Reprograms Your Mind

Pluto in Aquarius activates your House III all year long : your way of thinking, communicating and learning undergoes transformation. You release mental automatisms for more powerful, lasting visions, anchored in inner truth.

"Change your way of thinking, and you change your reality."

6. Key Phases of 2026

- **June–July** : Jupiter changes signs. The dynamic shifts from relationship to spiritual expansion.

- **July 20** : Jupiter–Neptune trine a window to dream big and set powerful intentions.

- **July 20–21** : Jupiter–Pluto opposition Jupiter–Uranus sextile you are torn between personal expansion and mental reorganization, yet a wind of renewal pushes you to cross a relational or professional threshold.

Bonus Advice

- Work on your partnerships : until June, the dynamic is fertile, but requires profound adjustments.

- Study or teach : the second half of the year is ideal for everything related to education, writing and philosophy.

- Clarify your foundations : Saturn and Neptune urge you not to build on sand.

- Welcome the unexpected : Uranus, twice this year, unleashes powerful liberations.

2026

A Year to Rewrite Your Story

Sagittarius, this year propels you into a more mature, more grounded yet freer version of yourself. The stars impose nothing they offer. It is up to you to say "yes" to what feels true.

"Dream big. Start small. Act now." Robin Sharma

Esoteric and Spiritual Synthesis

Energetic Correspondences

Astrology, Lithotherapy, Aromatherapy and Floral Symbolism

Sagittarius

- **Lucky Color** : Sapphire Blue – color of wisdom and spiritual expansion.

- **Stone to Wear** : Lapis Lazuli – stone of vision, truth and inner journey.

- **Essential Oil to Diffuse** : Frankincense (Olibanum) – opens access to higher planes and to philosophical intuition.

- **Inspiring Flower** : Iris – uplifts the spirit and invites nobility of soul.

"I aim for the stars, for my spirit is free and infinite."

Ruling Planets and Meaning

Sign	Ruling Planet	Symbolic Meaning
Sagittarius	Jupiter	Expansion, optimism, faith, exploration

Key Moments of Action in 2026

Sagittarius

- Jupiter in Sagittarius in December opens new perspectives.
- Eclipses in June and December stimulate personal growth.

Favorable Periods in Love

Sagittarius

- Until May 8 : Multiplication of opportunities to evolve love stories.
- November : A key discussion or decision redefining emotional priorities.
-

Favorable Periods Money and Work

Sagittarius

- Favorable period : All year.

- Planetary influence : The year favors careers linked to education, tourism or culture.

- Advice : Beware of imprudent spending despite a financially favorable year.

Favorable Periods Health and Well-being

Sagittarius

- Favorable period : All year.

- Planetary influence : The year favors careers linked to education, tourism or culture.

- Advice : Beware of imprudent spending despite a financially favorable year.

When the stars align to favor Luck, Miracles and Happy Surprises !

Sagittarius

- Favorable periods : June and December.

- Planetary influences :

  - Jupiter, your ruling planet, in a dominant position, fostering expansion and luck.

- ○ Mars in a favorable aspect, bringing energy and motivation.

- Advice : Pursue your goals with enthusiasm and optimism.

Spiritual Explanation

The "favorable periods", beyond the influence of the stars…

From all cultures, words resonate powerfully within this new cosmic frequency. When we choose joy, even in trial, we reset our inner vibration.

In the Age of Aquarius, faith becomes the key to quantum miracles. As Rumi said :

"What you seek is seeking you."

Thought creates, faith attracts and love elevates. Where our thoughts dwell, there lies our entire reality.

The Age of Aquarius is the age of awakened consciousness, of sharing Light, of faith in the Invisible and of the power of Heart and Will. It is an era in which humanity rediscovers that it is a co-creator of its reality, and that everything is possible, provided one truly wills it with faith, love and pure thoughts.

"The whole world is a very narrow bridge. The essential thing is never to be afraid."

"There is no despair in this world... Joy is not merely an emotion, it is a channel to the divine." Rabbi Nachman of Breslov

And Martin Luther King Jr. reminded us :

"Faith is taking the first step even when you don't see the whole staircase."

Everything becomes possible when the mind yields to the soul, when we cease to doubt and allow ourselves to dream big, to love without measure.

"I am as My servant thinks of Me." Hadith Qudsi, narrated by Al-Bukhari and Muslim

This sacred Hadith means that if you sincerely believe that God (Allah) reserves Good for you, grants you His mercy and answers your prayers, then He will act with you according to your trust in Him. It is a call to absolute faith, to positive thinking and to boundless hope.

Through faith, everything is transformed. Through love, everything is fulfilled.

In this new era, the inner sky is greater than ever. Believe, love, hope and let the Universe open its doors to you !

Love Compatibilities

Love is a mysterious alchemy guided by the stars…

Sagittarius

- Compatible with : Aries, Leo, Aquarius

- Why ? Free-spirited and enthusiastic, Sagittarius seeks a love that does not imprison but uplifts.

"To love is to prefer the other to oneself, without denying oneself in the process." Albert Einstein

Major Trends 2026

Sagittarius (November 23 – December 21)

"There is only one way to fail : it is to give up before succeeding." Georges Clemenceau

1st Decan (November 23 – December 2)

Doors open, new structures are put in place, and a field of possibilities presents itself to you. You have the opportunity to express yourself with greater freedom and authenticity, while remembering that lasting success requires time and method. Your ideal is taking shape, and it is up to you to find the balance between your highest aspirations and the rules necessary to achieve them.

"Patience is bitter, but its fruit is sweet." Aristotle

2nd Decan (December 3 – December 12)

Until May 8, 2026, Jupiter multiplies opportunities, whether in professional or romantic partnerships. Then, between August 14 and October 3, your ambitions take on a new dimension. Whether consolidating a love relationship, finding a soulmate or climbing the career ladder, everything seems possible !

"They did not know it was impossible, so they did it." Mark Twain

3rd Decan (December 13 – December 21)

The wind of change blows with even greater intensity in 2026. Between May 8 and June 30, external events stimulate your thirst for success. From October 3, 2026, you aspire more than ever to push your limits, whether by moving to new horizons or by accessing a higher position. Nothing can stop you !

"The future belongs to those who rise early." Benjamin Franklin

Intuitive Astrological Forecast 2026

For SAGITTARIUS

Month-by-Month

An illuminated year

A vibration to be lived

January — Sagittarius

Inner Ascension

Dazzling Awakening

Events do not always happen as you wish, so decide to want what happens and you will be happy.

The configurations in Capricorn until January 20 are your allies for examining with lucidity the structure of your resources and giving them both tangible and vibrational value. They invite you to make matter sing in resonance with the true pulsations of your heart. Saturnian influences exalt discernment : use them to bring your deepest aspirations to light.

From January 21, the entry of planets into Aquarius reorients your energy toward more intimate and communal spheres : siblings, neighborhood, soul tribes. An airy dynamic is woven into your exchanges, strengthening your radiance in social interactions. Intellect sharpens, listening becomes an art.

The home sector, still the subject of initiatory questioning, pushes you to strip away what no longer resonates with your inner peace. Fear not : this is a fertile pruning phase.

On January 26, Neptune enters Aries and touches the sanctuary of your emotional attachments. Love could then reveal itself as a subtle medicine, a balm for the soul.

"I love as love loves. I know no other reason to love than to love." Fernando Pessoa

Uranus, residing in the last decan of Taurus, electrifies your professional field. Expect breaks in patterns, unexpected bifurcations. Welcome them with grace : they will be springboards into a bolder, more efficient version of yourself.

Jupiter, in Cancer, operates in the sphere of savings and passive capital. Income from investments or external support can be favorably considered. Be receptive to flows of abundance.

LOVE

Until January 17, the conjunction of Venus and Mars in Capricorn intensifies your sensuality and desire for possession. Caution is advised : jealousy could overshadow the depth of the bond. Let love breathe so that it may reveal its highest truth.

From January 21, the element Air enters with Aquarius, facilitating stimulating encounters, sudden infatuations, sometimes tinged with idealistic romanticism.

"Love is the miracle of a translation : from solitude to communion." Christian Bobin

In a Relationship

A climate of complicity is established from the very first days of the month. Exchanges are solid, sometimes serious, sometimes adventurous, oscillating between rootedness and openness. Take care, however, not to give in to a desire for emotional control. Love is built on shared freedom, not on control disguised as attention.

Single

Your magnetism increases until January 17, fueled by a determination to love without pretenses. After the 21st, astral configurations favor a meaningful, foundational encounter. On January 26, Neptune enters the scene : you may meet a soul love, a vibration of the absolute !

"To love is to know how to say 'I love you' without speaking." Victor Hugo

Money and Work

Your eloquence, clear and incisive, works wonders throughout the month. Seize this period to negotiate, propose, reposition your ideas. Uranus, always seeking innovation, pushes you to abandon obsolete methods in order to align with solutions of the future. Adaptability will be your strength.

Jupiter invites you to structure and optimize your income. It is the right time to reassess your financial strategy or to invest in projects imbued with meaning.

Advice

Take your time ! Some questions, particularly within the home, require silence, gentleness and sincere listening. But know this : your gifts, your creative impulses and above all your capacity to love will have full scope to be expressed. Do not restrain them.

"Life is 10% what happens to you and 90% how you react to it." Charles R. Swindoll

Why should you believe in LUCK in January 2026 ?

Jupiter–Uranus Conjunction in Taurus (House VI)

In January 2026, Jupiter, traditional ruler of Sagittarius, forms an exact conjunction with Uranus in the sign of Taurus, located in your House VI (daily work, habits, health, method). This is an exceptional, rare aspect, heralding sudden breakthroughs and tangible opportunities.

For Sagittarius, this means the eruption of a major opportunity linked to a project built over time, often in a field where you did not expect to progress so quickly. This rewards audacity aligned with a stable vision, not irrational gambles. This is the moment when you must act to find your true place. Do not ask for it. Take it !

Mars in Capricorn (House II)

Mars, planet of action, crosses Capricorn in House II (values, personal finances, sense of security). This transit pushes you to assert your worth in concrete terms. This is not the time to doubt ! It is the time to show through actions that you know what you are worth.

Mars in Capricorn is strategic and rigorous, and its energy supports those who work with disciplined confidence. If you have an idea, a project, an ambition, this is the moment to materialize it !

North Node in Aries (House V)

The North Node, karmic indicator of personal evolution, transits your House V, that of creation, personal expression and passion projects. This is a clear call : you are meant to create, not to imitate. You are meant to step forward, even if it takes you out of your comfort zone. Doors will only open if you walk toward them with an uncompromising inner fire.

Conclusion

You do not need to wait for someone to give you permission. The planetary aspects of January 2026 send you a clear message : *"You are ready if you act as if you are."*

Luck does not manifest by waiting for signs. It takes shape in built audacity, in gestures aligned with your own vision. Doubt is only the natural shadow preceding the clearing.

So move forward. Not with caution, but with the certainty that your path is legitimate ! The stars do not promise they give the green light.

It is up to you to decree that your road deserves to exist simply because you decide to draw it.

February - Sagittarius

A Majestic Astral Epic !

Between revisiting family resonances and a social life in full effervescence, February propels you into a whirlwind of experiences as captivating as they are demanding.

Until the 18th, a planetary quintet in Aquarius (Sun, Mercury, Venus, Mars and Pluto) activates your House of exchanges and connections : you are strongly advised to explore new relational territories, to renew fraternal or friendly ties and above all to verbalize what lies dormant within you.

From the 4th, Uranus, planet of surprises and sudden reversals, may trigger professional events as unexpected as they are beneficial. A strategic repositioning or a dazzling opportunity cannot be ruled out.

Jupiter, benevolent in your financial sector, watches over your resources and favors the consolidation of your savings, particularly if you were born between December 3 and 12. However, the planet's retrogradation suggests re-examining certain past choices with discernment.

Love

Saturn and Neptune conjoined in Aries favor a sincere quest for emotional stability. You move forward with confidence, driven by a will to build on solid ground.

From the 18th, the Sun enters Pisces and joins Mercury and Venus in a nebulous family sector. Expect areas of shadow, unspoken tensions. You will need to deploy your art of patience and avoid direct confrontations until the 27th, a date favorable for clarification.

"Clarity is not born of what we imagine of the world, but of what we transform." Frantz Fanon

From the 1st to the 10th, the trio Venus, Mars and Pluto compose an astral symphony highly favorable to your emotional fulfillment. Your impulses are right, your charm works with finesse, and your romantic interactions budding or established find deep resonance.

From the 11th onward, the energies flowing from Pisces instill a more vaporous, less tangible atmosphere. You may be unsettled by ambiguous feelings or contradictory signals.

"Love is the poetry of the senses." Honoré de Balzac

In a Relationship

The first third of the month envelops you in tender and radiant complicity. Your shared laughter resonates like echoes of childhood and your intimacy seems blessed by a soft light. Beware, however, of some communication friction around February 6 : active listening and tender gestures will be enough to dispel misunderstandings.

"It is not love that unites beings, it is complicity." Marc Lévy

Single

Mars and Pluto intensify your aura : you embody magnetism that is both subtle and captivating, combined with rare emotional intelligence. This climate favors an unexpected encounter marked by originality and intellectual resonance.

Stay attentive between the 10th and the 14th : a soul freed from traditional codes may enter your sphere.

After February 14, your desire transforms into an aspiration for a lasting relationship. Do not compromise with your ideals. Respect them ! Honor them !

Money and Work

Your financial domain benefits from Jupiter's protection, but with its retrogradation, you will be invited to reassess certain investments or review your savings strategy. If well handled, this process could even increase your income.

From the 4th, a push from Uranus may radically reshape your professional landscape : a transfer, an unexpected offer or an innovative project are possible. Your responsiveness will make the difference.

After the 14th, a small cosmic gamble could smile on you ! Why not try (not the Devil !) a game of chance ? Still, remain measured.

Advice

The end of the month calls for stoicism. You will face some turbulence, but your solar temperament will illuminate the way. Rely on grounding, gentle discipline and meticulous planning.

"It is not the mountain we conquer, but ourselves." Edmund Hillary

Nothing is denied you, provided you remain faithful to your inner compass.

Health

Take care of yourself to endure this very special month !

- **First fortnight** : Vitality rising, morale high ! Thanks to planets in Aquarius, you are full of energy, motivated and mentally clear. Ideal for movement, adopting a healthy routine, refining your lifestyle. Mars supports you : measure your efforts, but move forward with confidence.

- **Second fortnight** : Change of rhythm. The passage of planets in Pisces makes you more sensitive and demands more rest. Listen to your body : slow down, recenter, sleep better. Avoid stress, excess and mental overload.

Advice :

Move gently, avoid burnout. Strengthen your immunity (sleep, herbal teas, rest). Practice meditation, writing, inner silence. Accept slowing down in order to bounce back better.

"The true journey is to travel within." André Gide

March - Sagittarius

Composing with the Invisible

From the very first days of the month, a subtle and persistent tension may be felt within your domestic sphere. The Sun and Mercury in Pisces, until March 20, form a delicate square to your solar sign, signaling a stormy emotional climate. Family or intimate exchanges, sometimes tinged with misunderstanding, risk eroding your usual serenity. Preserve your energy by staying away from unnecessary verbal jousts.

"It is not because things are difficult that we do not dare, it is because we do not dare that they are difficult." Seneca

On March 2, Mars joins Pisces, adding an impulsive note to your reactions. If an emotion overwhelms you, let it pass like a cloud : do not act in anger or haste. Rash action could cloud the accuracy of your choices. Pluto, meanwhile, offers you discreet yet powerful inner strength. Your morale, intact, guides you with dignity. Beware, however, of a temperament a little too directive : this month, an excess of lucidity may wound the sensitivities around you. Keep in mind that relational intelligence is a method of action, not a rigid demonstration.

From March 6, a saving turning point begins. The entry of Venus into Aries, then that of the Sun on March 21, re-enchants your loving, creative and spiritual impulses. This Fire dynamic, allied with your free and powerful Sagittarius nature, opens a new cycle of inspiration, passion and assumed audacity. Do not anticipate   let yourself be carried by the impulses of the heart.

"There is a crack in everything, that's how the light gets in." Leonard Cohen

This line evokes the idea that our flaws, wounds or imperfections are not weaknesses to be hidden, but passages through which clarity, truth and beneficial transformation may emerge.

Love

From March 6, Venus in Aries breathes into your heart a noble and incandescent flame ! Your sentimental impulses will be as powerful as they are authentic. Yet Mars in Pisces, from the 2nd, awakens disordered, anarchic desires. This dissonance can create inner conflict : reason of the heart versus impulse of the body. The task is to harmonize these forces without denying them. Listen to what you feel and what you truly desire.

"I do not ask you to love me always like this, but I ask you to remember. Somewhere inside me, there will always be someone waiting for you." Frida Kahlo

In a Relationship

Communication may falter before the 20th. Words spoken hastily, trivial misunderstandings may grow larger. Favor active listening   listening that understands without interrupting, that hears even silence. From the 6th, Venus rekindles the flame : you will feel more in love than ever, in a tender yet conquering intimacy. Your desires will dance with the lunar tides : variable but sincere. Cultivate tenderness more than possession.

"The secret of happiness in love is not to be blind, but to know how to close your eyes when necessary." Simone Signoret

Single

This month, your charm may be out of sync with your deeper intentions. Impulsiveness, clumsiness or haste risk blurring the message you want to convey. You could miss a promising encounter, not for lack of opportunity, but through impatience. Wait for clearer days, after March 21, to engage in sincere, aligned seduction.

"From now on I want only loves without traps." Barbara

Money and Work

Under the attentive eye of Jupiter, your ruling planet, the material and professional sphere is under strong protection. Notably, from March 11 onward, a sum or providential support could appear through a masculine figure or an institution (bank, advisor, lawyer…). If you are engaged in financial, legal or administrative matters, persevere : results promise to be fruitful. No major disturbances are expected regarding your financial stability.

"Luck is when talent meets opportunity." Pierre-Auguste Renoir

Advice

Do not try to control everything. Let go of what escapes you, especially at the beginning of the month, and focus on your emotional grounding. Your legitimacy will come from the calm you know how to maintain, not from the turmoil you attempt to master.

"Let things unfold. What you chase with persistence slips away. What you welcome comes to you." Lao Tzu

April - Sagittarius

The Heart Beats to the Rhythm of the Sky

A wild month

A new breath rises in your intimate sky : the planets in Aries, strongly positioned, activate your emotional sphere with warm, luminous intensity. Carried by this benevolent celestial conjunction, you bathe in a climate where hope, trust, the joy of loving and a subtle note of emotional lucidity coexist in harmony. This month is an invitation to open your heart fully, without losing your grounding.

Pluto, in a beneficial aspect, strengthens your morale and grants you serene poise. You feel a renewed inner clarity, as though your emotional compass were finally pointing in the right direction. Uranus, meanwhile, enters the scene on April 26, ready to shake up your relational or contractual ties. This transit may trigger a sudden encounter or an unexpected marital upheaval : transformation or revelation, it is up to you to sense what you are ready to welcome.

"The greatest strength of a loving heart is daring to be vulnerable." Brené Brown

On the material plane, Jupiter watches over your finances with indulgence. Your capital is protected, even enhanced. Why not indulge this month in a small game of chance ? Luck seems to linger around you…

Beware, however, between April 1 and 15, of a slight emotional haze in your domestic sphere. Your words could exceed your intentions : handle your interlocutors gently, especially in the family circle. Clarity will return from the 21st, with the entry of the Sun into Taurus, which stabilizes your daily life and favors your professional commitment.

Love

Your emotional life looks fulfilled and vibrant, carried by profoundly inspiring celestial configurations. Saturn and Neptune in Aries, in harmonious aspect with your sign, elevate your quest for love to a higher level of consciousness. You will no longer settle for half-measures : you seek a bond that is sincere, reciprocal, rooted in mutual respect and nourishment of the soul.

If you had a confession to make, a bond to strengthen or a truth to bring into the light, this month gives you the courage to do so.

In a Relationship

A somewhat turbulent start to the month may require you to show tact and kindness, especially on issues linked to your home or family circle (April 1–8). Guard against outbursts : loving listening is worth more than spontaneous reaction.

From the 6th, conjugal life ignites with joyful passion. Dialogue regains lightness, bodies seek each other, complicity is reborn. And on April 26, Uranus may blow an unprecedented surprise into your life as a couple : twist, revelation, or new soul-to-soul pact. Be ready to welcome the unexpected.

"True love is that which makes you a better person, without ever asking you to change." Frida Kahlo

Single

You enter a month both contrasting and electrifying. On one hand, a sincere quest for stability pushes you to commit, to seek a relationship with meaning. On the other, a breeze of carefreeness may tempt you to scatter, especially around April 24.

But it is especially on the 26th, under the impulse of Uranus, that the stars promise a dazzling encounter, out of the ordinary coup de foudre or unexpected revelation ! Be attentive to synchronicities. Love could appear where you least expected it.

"I love you without knowing how, or when, or from where. I love you simply, without problems or pride : I love you in this way because I do not know any other way of loving." Frida Kahlo

Money and Work

Rest assured : no storm looms on the financial horizon. On the contrary, Jupiter, in a supportive aspect, gives you the possibility to consolidate or even increase your assets. A significant inflow of money, coming from a partnership or ongoing contract, could materialize in the last week of the month.

This is also a month when the notion of personal value clarifies. You will know how to assert your skills with confidence, especially from the 21st, when the Sun in Taurus warms your sphere of daily work. Ground yourself in the concrete, advance step by step : your efforts will be rewarded.

"Success is going from failure to failure without losing enthusiasm." Winston Churchill

Advice

Do not yield to the temptation of self-glorification. Yes, things are working in your favor, but it is in elegant discretion and sincere sharing that you will magnify your April. Let life unfold, welcome destiny's gifts without trying to control them. True mastery is trust.

"There is no need to force the course of things, for what is destined for you will reach you." Eckhart Tolle

Focus for this Exceptional Month !

Neptune in Pisces (House IV) trine Venus in Cancer (House VIII)

April 2026 offers you a rare configuration : Neptune, planet of spiritual loves, compassion and soul bonds, transits Pisces, its own sign, in your House IV that

41

of roots, deep emotional intimacy, love that defies explanation.

Simultaneously, Venus crosses Cancer, in House VIII   the house of intimate bonds, emotional fusion and radical transformations through love.

The trine formed between these two planets opens a unique window : that of an unconditional, fusion-based, deeply healing love. This is not a fleeting romance. This is a soul-to-soul encounter, which invites Sagittarius, usually free and in motion, to invest its fire not in conquest, but in depth.

What this reveals about you, Sagittarius

You are often perceived as the traveler, the explorer of horizons. But this configuration reminds you of a forgotten truth : the greatest journey is sometimes the one undertaken in a single gaze, a single heart.

This love is not here to hold you back. It is here to make you vaster, to reconnect you to your capacity to love without reserve, without the need to flee, without fear of being burned. To love here is to become greater than yourself.

"I ask nothing of you. I love you as one opens a door that will never again be closed. I love you with what I am, with what I will become."

May - Sagittarius

Transitions
Opportunities
Constructive Vigilance

"There is no such thing as failure, only feedback."
Richard Bandler

Until May 21, thanks to the combined presence of the Sun and Mercury, you will be solicited in the professional domain. A considerable workload may be imposed on you, yet you will show efficiency. An important piece of news reaches you, or a significant change occurs. Do not let opportunities pass you by : they could transform your daily life if you act with discernment.

Between the 1st and the 18th, Mars, Saturn and Neptune will form an alignment favorable to your inspiration and creativity. If you belong to the 1st decan, you will be particularly sensitive to this influence : seize opportunities with spontaneity, but avoid charging ahead blindly. Your intuition will be precious, but it must be accompanied by strategy.

Your mindset, tinged with idealism and a desire for progress, will push you to reconsider certain habits. Jupiter will strengthen your material stability and may stimulate your sensory pleasures. This planetary support is ideal for laying down solid foundations, though prudence is required in commitments.

Until the 19th, Venus and Uranus, in good aspect, could trigger a surprising development in your couple life or in an important partnership. Stay open to the unexpected, especially if a couple decision or contract seems to evolve suddenly.

After the 19th, the pace of your days will intensify. Professionally, you will need to advance with method and rigor. Avoid haste : better one measured step than a false start.

"Everything you need is already within you, you just have to release it." Tony Robbins

This configuration is an invitation to draw from your inner resources, richer than you think.

From the 22nd, the planets in Gemini will orient you toward others. It will be an ideal period to strengthen your connections, both personal and professional, provided you show diplomacy.

Love

"I will love you to the end of silences." Alain Borne

You will feel a deep interest in emotional relationships and be willing to commit, if you haven't already. Uranus could trigger unexpected twists in your married life. Keep a flexible mind and adapt to change without dramatizing.

Until the 18th, your love energy will be lively, and you will radiate a magnetic presence. After this date, sensuality will take precedence : your desire will be powerful, in harmony with your feelings. Be attentive to emotional signals both yours and those of the other.

If you are in a relationship

Until the 19th, your relationship could benefit from unexpected renewal. This may take the form of a pleasant surprise or an unforeseen project shared with your partner. However, after this period, Venus may awaken a form of jealousy or possessiveness. A climate of trust will be essential to preserve the quality of the bond. Do not let misunderstandings take root.

If you are single

Between the 1st and the 18th, the stars will favor encounters. Your way of communicating will be particularly captivating, and you will radiate a magnetism that is hard to ignore. Toward the end of the month, an attraction could develop in a professional setting.

Money and Work

A key to letting go of fear and embracing change.

"What you resist persists. What you accept transforms." Carl Jung

This month, your financial sector benefits from the benevolence of Jupiter, joined by Venus from the 19th onward. A gain or positive material news may follow. Before this date, a contract revision or professional renegotiation could work in your favor. Examine every proposal carefully before signing anything.

"Change your thoughts and you change your world." Norman Vincent Peale

Advice

Our reality begins with the way we think. Your dynamism will be a true driving force. Launch yourself into what inspires you — be it a creative project, a new emotional bond, or a professional goal. The Universe is pushing you toward change ; be sure to remain lucid and centered. Some opportunities may be fleeting : learn to distinguish true riches from seductive mirages.

Rely on Your Intuitive Genius

Saturn in Pisces (House IV) sextile Uranus in Taurus (House VI)

This month, Saturn, planet of discernment, inner discipline and maturity, transits Pisces in Sagittarius' House IV : the house of the soul, invisible foundations, inner voice. In sextile to Uranus, planet of intuitive genius and awakening, in Taurus (House VI), the house of daily life, repeated acts and embodied work, a dynamic emerges :

- What you feel inside begins to translate clearly into your concrete choices.

- You effortlessly distinguish what uplifts you from what diverts you from your axis.

- It is not cold logic. It is not impulsive instinct. It is your inner compass, long refined, that begins to speak with authority.

Mercury in Taurus (House VI) trine Pluto in Aquarius (House III)

Your speech becomes sharper. You no longer speak to convince. You express what you know to be true. Pluto here makes you uncompromising toward the false, the vague, the compromised.

Moon in Scorpio (opposite Sun in Taurus) around mid-May

Emotionally, this Full Moon forces you to face what you feel but have not yet dared to act upon. It pushes you to choose what aligns, not what merely reassures.

Conclusion

May 2026 is a month when Sagittarius sees with clarity, but not with the eyes. They simply feel. They cut clean. They move straight ahead. It is a moment to continue trusting yourself calmly without agitation, without external validation.

"It is not because others doubt that you must doubt. Clarity does not need applause to exist." Carl Jung

June - Sagittarius

Dazzling Passage

Inner Revelation

Passionate Sparks

A month of subtle metamorphosis and relational awakening opens before you, marked by surprise, introspection and radiant charisma.

The Sun, anchored in the talkative constellation of Gemini until the 21st, and electrifying Uranus, resident all month, orchestrate a disconcerting celestial ballet in your sphere of commitments marriages, professional alliances, soul pacts. Unexpected upheavals, sometimes salvific, are taking shape. Stay vigilant around June 6, when the celestial configurations call for lucidity in the face of sudden reversals !

Mars, valiant in patient and sensual Taurus, enlivens your daily life with methodical energy. You will act with fruitful efficiency, combining endurance with practicality.

Saturn, Neptune and Pluto, in harmonic benevolence to your sign, offer you emotional, intellectual and creative grounding of rare density. Their action, subtle yet decisive, invites you to transmute old blockages. Around June 17, transcendent inspiration may arise, illuminating an essential decision.

The trio Mercury, Venus and Jupiter in Cancer until the 12th endows you with a captivating aura and a palpable magnetic sensuality. After the 22nd, your emotional expression will carry incandescent warmth, propitious to the ignition of hearts. Prepare for a month's end under the sign of exaltation.

Love

Blooming
Revelation
Discovery

"When you look at me, I become beautiful." Amedeo Modigliani

From June 1–12, you may feel deep emotional impulses but find them complex to verbalize. The language of tender gestures will prevail. Yet beware of slipping into gentle confusion. Your need for authenticity must remain audible.

From the 13th onward, the winds shift. Your sacred fire reclaims its place, and love regains its nobility in a warm, clear climate. This is the moment to dare.

In a Relationship

A Garden to Cultivate

If you are engaged in a union, June 2026 urges you to avoid existential questioning that would only sow unnecessary doubts. Prefer to demonstrate sincere love through concrete, sensitive and audacious acts.

Introduce a note of eccentricity, a spark of playful madness into your sentimental routine : an unexpected gesture, an improvised getaway… Your partner will only ask to be surprised.

Single

Intertwined Destinies

Your sky brims with insolent opportunities. Do not underestimate the magic of everyday life : an encounter may arise in the ordinary on a familiar sidewalk, at a vernissage, a concert, or a countryside fête…

After the 13th, Cupid himself seems to choose you as a privileged target. The atmosphere becomes intensely romantic, favorable to the blossoming of a sincere and passionate romance.

"There are encounters that are reunions."   Jean d'Ormesson

Money and Work

Expansion
Reward

This month, the professional sphere looks prosperous, bathed in the benefits of planets in Cancer. Expect rapid, intuitive development of your projects, especially those that make your heart vibrate.

"Fear knocks at the door. Courage rises to open. And behold : no one is there." Carl Gustav Jung

Fear is often but an illusion amplified by inaction. Discouragement is the shadow of a step not yet dared. The energy of doubt can be transmuted into decisive action. Discouragement cannot withstand movement.

"Your life expands or contracts in proportion to your courage." Anaïs Nin

A notable inflow of money could fuel an artistic or spiritual ambition you have long nurtured. From the 22nd onward, stay alert to a message, proposal or signature bearing abundance.

Warning for the 1st decan : a contract may conceal an unspoken detail. Read between the lines, especially around June 18.

"Success is never an accident. It is the fruit of commitment, perseverance, and love of what you do." Colin Powell

Advice

Inner Alchemy

"Do not fear going slowly, fear only standing still." Chinese proverb

If emotional overload overwhelms you a rare but possible phenomenon under these stormy skies grant yourself a space for breathing. Stop trying to understand everything immediately. Let go, welcome, refocus on the q u a l i t y   o f   y o u r   b o n d s . Your relational wealth is your compass in this month of light.

Health

Key Transit : Mars in Leo (House IX) square Saturn in Pisces (House IV)

In June 2026, Mars, planet of vital energy, transits Leo, a fire sign like yours, activating your House IX convictions, ideals, meaning. This transit brings you a surge of energy, a need for movement, to go out, create, defend your ideas in short, to be fully alive !

But Mars forms a square with Saturn in House IV (the inner sphere, roots, bodily memory). This conflict between impulse and structural restraint may manifest as :

- Nervous fatigue or muscular tension if you push without listening to your rhythms.

- Too much inner fire, poorly channeled = inflammation, impatience, disturbed sleep.

- Possibility of finding a great renewal of energy if you respect your own bodily cycles instead of following external agendas.

This is a month when the body speaks clearly. Ignoring its messages would be a mistake.

Subtle Support : Venus in Cancer (House VIII) Emotional Healing

At the same time, Venus in House VIII brings soothing : if you connect to your deep emotions, you access a form of regeneration. Taking care of yourself here is not slowing down it is accessing a gentler, more enduring strength.

What this means for your health

In June, your health depends less on what you do than on the awareness with which you do it. It is not about slowing down, but about acting in alignment making fire rhyme with self-respect.

53

The Sagittarius who wants to ignite everything must learn to breathe between two gallops. That is where fire becomes sustainable.

"True strength is not moving fast, but knowing when to stop to hear what your body is trying to tell you."

July - Sagittarius

Inner Passage

High Vibrations

Good Voltage

"Where light enters, the shadow reveals its truth." Khalil Gibran

An emotional effervescence of rare intensity enters your relational universe, shaking your certainties and calling you toward a salutary introspective dive. Until July 22, the astral ballet orchestrated by the planets in Cancer magnifies your inner radiance and sharpens your quest for transparency. Expect hidden truths to rise, like pearls from the depths. Revelations may unsettle you, but you will feel guided toward lucid awakening.

Opposing your sky, Mars and Uranus stir palpable tension in your contractual or marital relations : the partnership zone becomes a theater of the unexpected and uncontrollable surprises. Possible friction or reversals of situation will push you to review your commitments with clarity. Prudence is advised until July 8, when Venus and Jupiter, in luminous conjunction, open a wide window of expansion. Rely on this alliance to broaden your emotional and spiritual horizons : your life ideal begins to materialize with clarity.

From the 9th onward, Venus sliding into Virgo soothes the professional atmosphere : harmonious collaborations could unfold, or your relational finesse could prove strikingly effective. An energy turned toward the future rises at the end of the month : lift your gaze, the time has come to dream big.

Love

"To love is to know how to say I love you without speaking." Victor Hugo

Your ardent sensitivity could play tricks on you if you neglect the codes of delicacy. The month begins under a passionate and demanding sky : facing you, the other will grant no indulgence to lapses of tact or elegance. Until July 8, your emotional impulses carry a vibrant joy, making your charm irresistible.

However, your electric sensuality could become a source of misunderstanding if you do not take care to channel your impulses. Ask yourself this essential question : do you seek to conquer or to share ?

In a Relationship

A highly volatile month, where the home can become the ground of a cold war. The celestial confrontation Mars–Uranus opposite your sign sparks belligerent sparks. It is crucial to defuse tensions before July 8, or a lasting escalation could settle in. Dialogue, nourished with kindness, will be your peaceful weapon. Cultivate the art of verbalization.

Advice

Do not confuse passion with domination. Freedom is learned together, too.

Single

An intriguing encounter could disrupt your daily life : a vibrant being, with elusive energy, enters your magnetic field. This bond, as exhilarating as it is unpredictable, invites you to question your deepest desires.

Your way of communicating will need to be more caress than arrow : measure your words, wrap them in softness. After July 9, the professional setting could become a stage of seduction : stay attentive to lingering glances and eloquent silences.

"I love you in an irrational, inconceivable, indomitable way... Like a storm that does not seek to be loved in return." Frida Kahlo

Money and Work

A decisive announcement, verbal or written, will impact your finances from July 23 onward. You will then have the combative energy needed to begin negotiations or revise agreements without confusing determination with aggression.

"The art of persuasion is the art of not forcing." Lao Tzu

Your assets seem protected, yet events push you to redefine your strategy for prosperity. Vigilance and diplomacy will be your allies.

Advice

Expect a month punctuated by unexpected reversals and cosmic surprises. Your nomadic and daring nature will revel in it : you do not flee change, you summon it. Welcome the unforeseen as a gift from the Universe.

"It is not the wind that decides your destination, it is the orientation you give your sails." Jim Rohn

Focus

August 2026 : A Shock, a Response, a Victory

Phase of Imbalance : Mars in Virgo square Jupiter in Gemini

"We do not fight to prove we are strong. We fight because we know we are worthy of respect." Brené Brown

From the first week of August 2026, Mars enters Virgo (House X for Sagittarius), squaring Jupiter in Gemini (House VII). This square triggers a frontal conflict between the drive for concrete action (Mars in Virgo) and the expectations of others or partnerships (Jupiter in VII).

Concretely :

- Unexpected attacks or criticism in the professional or relational sphere.

- The impression that your efforts are misunderstood or sabotaged.

- The feeling of having to justify yourself under external pressure, when you thought you had control.

- You may be surprised, misinterpreted, or destabilized.

"Defending oneself is not attacking. It is standing tall, calmly, in what one knows to be just." Alexandra Elle

This is precisely where Sagittarius will turn trial into leverage.

Sagittarius' Capacity to Defend Themselves

Victory !

Mercury in Leo trine Chiron in Aries

From mid-August, Mercury in Leo (House IX) forms a powerful trine with Chiron in Aries (House V). This reactivates in you the power of the word, personal faith, the ability to assert your singular voice even under pressure.

This trine makes you :

- Clear in your intentions.

- Brilliant in your responses.

- Proud without rigidity.

You no longer react with violence. You set your limits with elegance. Above all, you turn pressure into a source of creativity and affirmation.

Strategic Turning Point of the Month : Sun in Leo sextile Mars

Around August 20, the Sun (in Leo, House IX) enters sextile with Mars : you regain your fire. You act with conviction that commands respect. You no longer seek to prove. You show.

Conclusion

Sagittarius does not let themselves be brought down. They rise. Imbalance tests you. Your inner truth straightens you. Your expressive strength protects you.

"It is not what happens to you that defines you, it is what you make of it." Viktor Frankl

August - Sagittarius

Expansion and Revelations

The month of August unfolds like a chiaroscuro fresco, mingling concrete advances and essential adjustments. Under the Sun in Leo until the 23rd, your quest for elevation   whether geographical, spiritual or administrative   benefits from a radiance conducive to the realization of your ideals. If you have envisioned a project abroad, an official procedure, or a life reorientation, now is the time to plant the seeds of the future.

Between the 10th and the 24th, Mercury distills fertile energy in the form of news with high potential for evolution. You may receive information or encounter an opportunity that colors your summer with hope and bright promise. Your morale is strong, particularly for the 1st decan, reinforced by an associative or contractual life punctuated with galvanizing and encouraging twists.

From the 11th, Mars amplifies your magnetic aura and awakens in you a desire for truth, an intimate quest where buried secrets could surface with disconcerting ease. The realm of creation, love and personal expression takes on a will for stability, like a sudden urge to build something lasting, solid, rooted.

From the 24th onward, the entry of the Sun and Mercury into Virgo heralds unmistakably the return to discipline : the rentrée approaches with its share of responsibilities, as well as opportunities to seize in the concrete.

"The greatest traveler is not the one who goes ten times around the world, but the one who goes once around himself." Confucius

Love

Sensitivity and Rebirth

Until August 5, your emotions rise to the surface of your awareness. This hypersensitivity may destabilize you : allow yourself to be carried without resistance, without trying to control. Welcome the sweetness of spontaneous, frank, sacred sensuality.

From the 6th onward, Venus releases in you a breath of exalted, joyful, childlike love. However, until the 10th, Mars and Uranus ignite conflictual sparks in your relationships : disagreements, misunderstandings or ego clashes could arise. Wait until the 11th to fully feel the surge of the senses and the sincerity of the heart.

In a Relationship

Reconnection, Tensions

The first decade of the month (1st–10th) looks tense if you do not take care with your tone or silences. Your partner may voice needs or desires you have neglected. Adapt. Refusing dialogue would open the door to a cold war.

After the 11th, tensions dissipate and lightness returns, without diminishing the intensity of your desires. Seek harmony in authenticity and shared tenderness.

"Love does not consist in saying you love each other, but in living it in the silence of the obvious." Paul Éluard

Single

A Defining Encounter

A significant encounter may arise, particularly for the 1st and 2nd decans, with a person of great soul maturity or older than you. This connection could be gentle, instructive and deeply transformative.

Between the 10th and the 24th, Mercury endows you with elegant speech and refined wit : fertile ground for an intelligent, magnetic, playful flirt. Do not let pass a soul that touches you : your humor and lucidity will strike home.

"There is no love, there are only proofs of love." Jean Cocteau

Money and Work

Transition
Precautions

Your professional sky may undergo significant reshuffling: a revised contract, a transformed partnership, or a sudden change of direction, influenced by Mars and Uranus until the 10th. Tensions are not excluded, whether they come from within or from external forces. It will be salutary to bide your time, use diplomacy, and aim for fairness.

From the 10th to the 24th, the celestial configuration becomes more favorable to calm, constructive dialogue. Act without haste, with faith in your vision.

"Success belongs to those who see far without losing sight of the present." Jim Rohn

Health

Balance and Grounding

Digestive vigilance is required: the Virgo influences at the end of the month remind you that the body is a temple to be respected. Hydrate, breathe, and ensure restorative sleep to preserve your natural momentum.

Advice

Let yourself be carried by enthusiasm without being swept away. August calls you to balance expansion with recentring. After the 6th, friendships will be precious and your creative impulses nourished by stimulating presences. Do not resist the call of joy, learn to anchor it in reality.

"One does not become light without burning a little of oneself." Carl Gustav Jung

Sagittarius - September

Alchemy of Possibilities

Power of Discernment

This month of September opens on a dynamic of concrete transformation, carried by the powerful auspices of the Sun in Virgo until the 22nd, joined by Mercury until the 9th and framed by the driving influence of Mars. This planetary triptych invites you to revisit your professional ambitions and to transmute financial concerns into lucid, calibrated, strategic action.

Virgo's energies summon you to act with discernment, to reform your work habits, or to redefine your material value. You are called to reclaim mastery over your resources with intelligence, clarity and firmness.

"Discipline is the bridge between dreams and their realization." Jim Rohn

Uranus, in direct opposition for first-decan natives, may crack a contract, disrupt an alliance, or overturn a promise. The unexpected will be your means of learning. Welcome this jolt as a chance to evolve. Adapt flexibly or refrain from advancing.

Fortunately, Jupiter, ruler of your sign, watches over you like a lighthouse in the fog. It illuminates your great ambitions: a project abroad, a high-level administrative step, or higher learning imbued with meaning. Seize this springboard between the 10th and the 28th, when Mars joins Jupiter, galvanizing your capacity for bold, inspired action.

From the 23rd, the Sun slips into Libra, joined by Mercury. The sky opens to social harmony: fruitful encounters, precious friendships, luminous collaborations. You may weave a bond within a single conversation.

"Meeting is the sacred act of two paths that recognize each other." Clarissa Pinkola Estés

Love

Truth and Unspoken Words

Until the 9th, your heart vibrates within the friendship and emotional sphere. A gentle affection could turn into desire, a platonic bond into tender intimacy. Your sensuality reaches burning heights until the 27th, guided by the earthy influence of Mars.

But from the 10th, Venus enters Scorpio, tinting your impulses with mystery, intensity and silence. You feel with depth, yet the expression of your emotions collides with an inner reserve. Those around you may remain unaware of your secret storms. This gap could trouble the flow of exchanges: stay vigilant.

"Silence is sometimes the most beautiful declaration of love." Salvador Dalí

In a Relationship

Between Fire and Shadows

Your shared life breathes freedom and sensuality. This cocktail can revitalize your exchanges, yet stir insecurities in your partner. If there are unspoken truths or longings for elsewhere, open a peaceful dialogue. Do not let fantasies disrupt real love.

"To love is to know how to say without speaking what the other guesses without hearing." Victor Hugo

Single

Loving Freedom and Whispered Secrets

Your natural magnetism radiates all month, and your physical energy drives you to multiply impulses without immediate desire for attachment. Love scatters, flutters, experiments… until, at the end of the month, a more secret or atypical bond settles behind the scenes.

Do not trust appearances : behind a glance or a silence may lie an unexplored depth.

"The heart has its labyrinths that reason cannot map." Frida Kahlo

Money and Work

Reward

Until the 22nd, you travel through a landscape dotted with professional adjustments. A contract may be renegotiated, a partnership shaken, or a new income model considered. These tensions are not obstacles, but invitations to reinforce your professional sovereignty.

Your financial instinct will be sharp until the 27th, which could result in a welcome inflow of money provided you do not rush into agreements without solid foundations. Avoid promising more than you can deliver.

"Patience is bitter, but its fruit is sweet." Jean-Jacques Rousseau

Health

Your digestive system may be sensitive: adopt a simple diet and avoid excess toward the end of the month. Take care of your nerves and your sleep: a mental pause or silent retreat would do you great good.

Advice

Combine rigor with faith, strategy with intuition. The sky confronts you with decisive choices, equipping you to respond with wisdom and flair. Do not let impatience undermine your efforts: what you build in today's silence will be tomorrow's strength.

"The greatness of man lies in his ability to transform shadow into light." Carl Gustav Jung

Sagittarius - October

Secret Resonances

Unfolding

This month of October weaves around you a subtle fabric, made of worldly light and intimate shadows. The Libra energies the Sun until the 22nd and Venus from the 25th place you at the heart of the relational sphere. Your aura shines in social circles, your ideas seduce, your presence reassures. The time is ripe for enriching encounters, cooperative projects, elective connections.

Mercury, in discreet station all month, and Venus, silent until the 24th, signal a deep inner retreat, a need for chosen silence, for affective meditation. You will speak only when necessary, with the rare nobility of those who have mastered their inner world. Your emotional life may cloak itself in precious discretion, away from eyes and rumors.

"Silence is the greatest power of transformation." Lao Tzu

In parallel, Mars and Jupiter in Leo magnify your thirst for elsewhere, for ideal, for grandeur. Whether a journey, a project of expansion, or personal achievement, you are urged to aim beyond the horizon with ardor and nobility.

Pluto, for the 1st decan, exalts your psychic strength, charisma and inner faith. Your confidence is not noisy; it is unshakable. You are master of yourself, and that changes everything.

Finally, Uranus, still in direct aspect to the 1st decan, may rekindle a dormant relationship, whether intimate or professional. An old bond, forgotten or suspended, may resurface with renewed intensity.

After the 23rd, you enter a phase of observation: you listen more than you speak, you see without being seen. Your discernment becomes your greatest strength.

"What one sees depends on what one looks at and where one looks from." Henri Cartier-Bresson

Love

Secrecy and Intensity

The emotional climate of this month invites discretion, mystery, subtle awakening. A budding sentiment sheltered from view, or an old attachment reawakened, could overturn your certainties. Perhaps even a friend, silently, makes your heart beat.

Your sensuality, incandescent until the 27th, fuels your deepest desires. And from the 25th, Venus envelops you with tender, magnetic charm, making you as attractive as you are unreachable.

"The deepest love is often the one we never dare to speak." Claude Debussy

In a Relationship

Passion, Precaution

Your conjugal life could experience sharp surges of passion, provided you do not let jealousy undermine trust. Between the 1st and the 24th, rely on your inner fire, on vibrant sensuality to nourish intimacy and fortify complicity.

From the 25th, become the gentle poet of your relationship: tender gestures, chosen words, sincere attentions. Love is cultivated in detail, in listening, in pure intention.

"There is only one kind of love, but there are a thousand imitations." François de La Rochefoucauld

Single

Sublime Aspiration

You aspire to the unique, to great love, to the encounter that elevates the soul as much as the heart. Do not fall into the trap of scattered charm or seduction without commitment: your quest is noble and deserves to be honored.

Express your feelings sincerely, even if intensity frightens you. The fear of love does not protect, it isolates.

"True love begins where it expects nothing in return." Antoine de Saint-Exupéry

Money and Work

Invention

Professionally, the atmosphere is serene, without chaos or major upheaval. Yet Uranus, still active in the 1st decan's sky, could provoke a turnaround in a contract or alliance. It is essential to remain responsive, diplomatic, and fair.

Stay open to the unexpected: an original proposal may emerge where you least expect it. Your flexibility will be your best ally.

"There is no evolution without change, no progress without questioning." Robin Sharma

Health

Take care not to be overwhelmed by emotional overflow : your inner world will be dense, intense, powerful. Allow yourself silent pauses, far from screens, close to nature. Nervous system support and improved sleep quality will be essential allies.

Advice

This month is an invitation to connect deeply with your personal faith, with that little spark of hope that nothing can extinguish. Surround yourself with luminous people, do not fear retreat in order to hear the voice of the heart. What you nourish in silence today will shine tomorrow like a diamond.

"Nourish your inner light in secret, it will become a sun for the world." Yogi Bhajan

Spotlight

October 2026: The Moment of Sagittarius' Inner Ascension

"What you seek is seeking you." Rumi

1. **Jupiter (ruler of Sagittarius) in Cancer – Trine to Neptune in Pisces**

Jupiter, your ruling planet, is exalted in Cancer, a sign of intuition, protection, and inner expansion. It forms a harmonious trine with Neptune in Pisces, in your 4th house: that of deep roots, memory, and psychic security.

You are urged to become the truest version of yourself not by forcing, but by recognizing the legitimacy of your feelings and your inner vision ! Excellence is no longer performance. It becomes a natural radiance.

"You do not have to shine brighter than others. You have to shine exactly at your own frequency." Alexandre Jollien

2. **Mars in Sagittarius Conjunct the South Node – Sextile to Pluto**

Mars transits your sign and touches the South Node, karmic memory, past lessons, in sextile to Pluto in Aquarius (3rd house). This marks a crucial passage: you free yourself from old, ineffective patterns of action, from sterile restlessness, to enter a mastered power.

No longer needing to scatter your energy, you embody a clear, precise, focused direction. You are ready to act calmly but with no turning back.

3. **Mercury in Libra Trine Saturn in Gemini (7th house)**

Your way of thinking and expressing yourself gains maturity, weight, and quiet authority. This transit allows you to ground your ideas in solid alliances, lasting commitments, enlightened communications.

You become a bridge between the ideal and the concrete.

Conclusion

Sagittarius moves toward excellence!

"Excellence is not an act, it is a habit." Aristotle

This October 2026 asks you to believe in a version of yourself that no longer needs to force. Your excellence comes from alignment, not from tension. It comes from the full acceptance of who you are, with all your flames and silences.

"Self-mastery is not self-restraint. It is no longer needing to prove yourself." — Frédéric Lenoir

Sagittarius - November

Inner Renaissance

Expansion

This month of November opens under the seal of inner reconquest! Until the 22nd, you are invited summoned to a face-to-face with yourself. The Sun in Scorpio illuminates the zones of your unconscious. Mercury, present throughout the month, facilitates a powerful, almost alchemical introspection, whose concrete fruits may emerge around the 13th.

This moment of intimacy with your mind is not withdrawal, but renewal. A vibrational restructuring. In silence, you are preparing for a blazing takeoff!

From the 1st to the 24th, Mars and Jupiter in Leo ignite your impulses for action: an initiatory journey, a seminar of study, or the founding of a higher life ideal may emerge as an obvious choice. Now is the time to aim for the summit, for the sky supports the bold with pure hearts!

From the 25th onward, action shifts to the professional field: your dynamism takes root in efficiency beware of confusing ambition with haste!

Uranus (1st decan) shakes the foundations of your contracts or intimate relationships. Unexpected events are to be anticipated: take them as heralds, not as threats.

Fortunately, Pluto watches over you, and through it, your circle supports you with rare loyalty. Your morale is unshakable, your faith in the future renewed.

75

After the 14th, a collective, associative, or activist project could take shape. Friends will be powerful allies, mirrors of your soul. And on the 23rd, the Sun finally enters your sign: happy birthday, and above all... shine without restraint!

"The inner fire, if cultivated, always ends up lighting the world." Pierre Teilhard de Chardin

Love

Challenge
Attachment
Freedom

Your heart longs for an anchor, for vibrant fidelity, but the sky sings you another song: that of the unexpected. Uranus shakes your emotional bearings, awakening desires, emotions, or buried questions.

Meanwhile, Saturn and Neptune work in silence to purify your bonds, allowing only true, lasting, honest loves to remain. Love becomes rare   but when it comes, it transcends!

Your ties take on a fraternal, friendly, gentle hue, where commitment is less a cage than an elevation.

"Love, when it is true, does not bind you. It sets you free." Khalil Gibran

In a Relationship

Different Rhythms, Essential Listening

Your thirst for movement, open air, outings with friends may symbolically or concretely distance you from your partner. This does not mean "disaffection," but simply "different tempo."

Dialogue with transparency: a misunderstood silence could create unnecessary distance. If not fusion, be deeply present to one another.

Single

Surprise, Destiny, Openness

If you accept letting go of control, life may offer you an encounter as original as it is unexpected! This will not be a banal love, perhaps a soul shock, born of a vibrant friendship or a deep exchange with someone from another horizon.

Open your arms to the unknown, without getting lost in scenarios. Let yourself be carried. Let yourself be loved!

"You touched me without taking me, and yet I remained within your light." Barbara

Money and Work

Strategic Redeployment

Vigilance

The professional climate seems stable, but it would be unwise to believe everything is fixed. For the 1st decan, Uranus may provoke a reversal in a contract or partnership. This is no evil: it is an opportunity to rebalance your interests.

From the 1st to the 24th, Mars and Jupiter support you powerfully in the legal or administrative field. Use this time to regularize a situation, clarify a commitment.

From the 25th onward, Mars stirs your ambition but also your impulsiveness. Beware of conflicts: favor strategy over confrontation.

"He who sees the wind turn does not worry, he hoists his sails differently." Tibetan proverb

Health

You need deep rest, to nourish your inner world as much as your body. Choose conscious solitude, gentle care, deep breathing. Your mental strength will do the rest.

Advice

This month, take the time to dream rightly. It is not yet time for frontal action, but for structuring within you the foundations of a higher vision. Dare! What you initiate in silence today will become tomorrow's certainty.

"Before conquering the world, conquer your own inner kingdom." Seneca

Sagittarius — December

Assertion
Clarity
Long-Term Vision

The last month of the year sees you stepping to center stage with panache! Until the 21st, the Sun illuminates your sign, supported by Mercury from the 6th to the 25th, infusing you with the vital drive to assert your values, intentions, and uniqueness aloud. You are inspired, direct, precise, and no longer tolerate compromise where truth must be proclaimed.

Your words, carried by a fiery breath, are powerfully effective! Do not confuse spontaneity with haste.

On the professional front, Mars in Virgo, an implacable strategist, electrifies your destiny sector. You are incisive, tenacious, surgical in your actions. Your ambition is noble remember not to forget flexibility in your exchanges.

"It is not strength, but perseverance that accomplishes great works." Samuel Johnson

Uranus (1st decan) plays the role of electroshock in the domain of contracts, alliances, or relationships: a sudden change, a reversal, or a realization could upend existing balances. Be attentive to the reactions of a partner or associate and favor diplomacy without betraying your principles.

Meanwhile, Jupiter strongly supports all administrative, legal, or visionary initiatives. It opens doors as long as you know which ones to knock on with conviction.

In the depths, Saturn, Neptune, and Pluto work in secret: they consolidate your emotional roots, mature your relational projects, and repair what is worthy of repair. You aspire to what is lasting, true, solid.

From the 22nd onward, your thoughts naturally turn to possessions, income, financial security. You enter a phase of material consolidation and reevaluation of your priorities.

"What you plant now, you will harvest later." Og Mandino

Love

Fire
Patience

From December 4th, Venus enters a phase of interiorization in your sky: your affective impulses become discreet, deep, at times difficult to verbalize. In parallel, Mars fuels a passionate, imperious libido.

You find yourself caught between intense desire and the difficulty of expressing emotion. The key? Patience, maturity, alignment of body, heart, and spirit.

"What cannot be said must be written, sung, or allowed to vibrate in a gaze." Édith Piaf

In a Relationship

Adjustments, Tender Listening

This month may carry some conjugal turbulence, especially if your partner feels a lack of attention or listening. Between the 6th and the 25th, Mercury supports you: show transparency, tact, emotional availability.

If you appear too reserved or absorbed in personal affairs, complicity could erode. Stay tender, even in silence.

"To love is to understand without speaking, to share without noise, to give without losing oneself." Marc Levy

Single

Dynamic Charm, Tamed Heart

Your desire to meet someone is real, palpable, energetic. Opportunities for flirtation or connections may arise through cultural, artistic, or playful outings. From the 4th onward, however, your emotions seem to retreat into slumber. You may charm, you may shine, but your heart feels suspended waiting for meaning more than conquest. Stay spontaneous, but do not feign an interest you do not truly feel.

"One seduces best not by seeking to seduce, but by seeking to reveal oneself." Henri Matisse

Money and Work

Clarity
Expansion

Your professional stance is assertive, strategic, direct. You radiate through your efficiency and your commitment. Take care not to wound certain sensitivities around you   colleagues, superiors, partners   as your intensity could be misinterpreted.

Uranus (1st decan) may alter a contract, introduce a new clause, a different opportunity, or even a rupture of agreement. Be attentive to legal details and negotiate with finesse.

On the financial side, the stars announce reinforced stability and even a significant increase at the end of the month, if you know how to capitalize on your recent gains.

"Success is the ability to go from one failure to another with no loss of enthusiasm." Winston Churchill

Health

Your energy level is high; beware of nervous exhaustion from mental overload. Allow yourself moments of silence, walks, longer nights of rest. The clarity of your mind will come through the peace of your body.

Advice

This year's end has the aura of a sacred reckoning! You stand at the crossroads between who you have been, who you have become, and who you are ready to embody. Exercise lucidity, balance, and fidelity to your ideals. Promise only what you can fulfill yet dare to dream higher than ever!

"Align with your soul, and the Universe will take care of the rest." Deepak Chopra

Dear Sagittarians,

At this close of 2026, allow me to extend my warmest, brightest, most benevolent wishes: may your Christmas be as sweet as a heart at peace, and may 2027 rise to the height of your sacred fire!

You have crossed the year 2026 with admirable strength, constant motivation, and unwavering faith in your ideals. Despite turbulence, inner challenges, and necessary readjustments, you never turned away from evolution — and that deserves to be honored. Bravo for your courage, your tenacity, and above all, for your ability to always aim higher!

Preview of Your 2027

Here are five major pillars shaping your astral sky in 2027:

- A bold reorientation in your life projects: a turn may impose itself, but you will have the courage to choose the true path.

- A precious stabilization in love: what you sow with authenticity will bear lasting fruit.

- Unexpected professional elevations: Uranus and Jupiter could spark positive surprises in your ambitions.

- A blazing spiritual and personal development: you will find answers you have long been seeking.

- An amplified social radiance: friends, networks, collaborations — you become a source of inspiration to others.

2027 will be a year of inner alignment, concrete manifestation, and measured expansion. The Universe supports you in making shine what is noblest within you.

"A life is not important except in the impact it has on other lives." Jackie Robinson

Karmic Plan 2026

Inspired by the influence of the North Node in Pisces and the South Node in Virgo (until July 2026). This cycle calls us to release rigidity, fear of error, and the need for control in order to embrace intuition, unconditional love, and transcendence.

The Call of the Lunar Nodes 2026

- **South Node in Virgo:** represents karma to be transcended reflexes of control, judgment, fear of disorder, hyper-analysis.

- **North Node in Pisces:** symbolizes the path of elevation welcoming intuition, faith, artistic inspiration, compassion, surrender.

Universal advice :

"Transformation begins the day you stop fighting against yourself." Debbie Ford

Sagittarius

Karmic Challenge

Release the outer quest for meaning at the expense of the heart's reality. You search too far for what is already here.

Path of Evolution

Invest in human warmth, home, shared emotions. Love is a field of growth.

Advice

Offer your presence to loved ones without agenda. Deep listening is a silent prayer.

"Love is a sanctuary built in daily life." Christiane Singer

Warning

Around June 6th, beware of unrealistic ideals. Foundations matter more than heights.

Mini Card Reading 2026

Sagittarius – Card: The Star of Man

Coaching:

"Be yourself; everyone else is already taken." Oscar Wilde

"I am the keeper of the sacred fire." Jean Cocteau

Message: A celestial energy propels you toward accomplishment. Be faithful to your essence.

The Angel whispers:

"The Universe leans where you place your faith."

Numerology 2026

Under the vibration of a **Year 1**

The 1 is a year of **INITIATIVE**.

Whatever your sign, the Universe asks you: *"What are you ready to begin in order to change your life?"*

Sagittarius

A year of total expansion.

A new journey, a renewed faith, an unprecedented adventure calls you! Year 1 is your field of exploration. You open doors to new horizons perhaps even beyond borders, or in the spiritual realm.

I wish you a 2026 rich in meaning, inner peace, and visible and invisible blessings. May you walk with confidence and joy upon this sacred path that is uniquely yours yet which, fundamentally, connects us all.

A beautiful year 2026 begins for Sagittarius, **TO SET GOALS BEYOND OUR LIMITS**

Rachel

RACHEL

Seer, Author, Artist, Spiritual Guide

t +33 6 26 86 77 21

R 10 Rue de la Radue, 69500 BRON, France

Ŭ Rachelnews@yahoo.fr

ɘ Rachel-conseils.com

By appointment only (in person or remote)

Available Services*: Clairvoyance, Life Coaching, Personalized Guidance, Original Artwork*
Availability: 7 days/week, afternoons & evenings
Appointments: +33 4 78 62 20 15 / +33 6 26 86 77 21

Media Presence*:*

Ẓ Daily horoscopes – Radio Scoop, Max Radio, Impact FM

* ̄ Live clairvoyance sessions – Sundays 12–2 PM*
ẑ Weekly replays – Thursdays on YouTube and Facebook
ɛ̇ YouTube: Rachel Levy

ṣ Facebook: Rachel Radio Scoop

. TikTok: @RACHELOFFICIEL2022

Published Works:

- *Murs d'Eau (Plon)*

- *Les Amants Terribles (Éditions Bélier)*

- *Les Voix (Aléas Publisher)*

Upcoming:

- *Murs d'Eau 2: One Soul for Two*

- *The Rachel Tarot (78 illustrated cards)*

Rachel's Signature:

With passion, candor, and love, Rachel speaks from Soul to Soul. She doesn't impose she illuminates. She doesn't dictate, she walks beside you. Always aligned. Always wholehearted.

INTUITIVE ASTROLOGICAL FORECAST 2026 – RACHEL
REBIRTH OF LOVE

2026 isn't just another year, it opens a Portal: the Rebirth of Love. Not romantic ornamentation, but Love as a foundational law of Life. Through Astrology, Intuition, Numerology, and even Quantum Physics, a clear message resonates: Love is returning. Transformative, guiding, liberating Love.

A multidimensional guide for an extraordinary year.
It replaces nothing it clarifies. It commands nothing it supports.

Each month, each frequency, each cosmic alignment is decoded to help you stay attuned to your highest potential.

You'll find key dates, practical advice, inspiring quotes, and luminous insights guiding you back to trust, to clarity, to your Self.

WELCOME TO 2026.

WELCOME TO YOUR REBIRTH. WELCOME TO THE YEAR WHERE IT ALL BEGINS.

Manufactured by Amazon.ca
Acheson, AB

30509874R00055